Bibliography

Share books depicting children and families from a variety of countries and cultures, using both fiction and nonfiction. Here are some suggestions to get you started.

Fiction:

Someday With My Father by Helen Buckley; Harper & Row, 1985
You Be Me I'll Be You by Pili Mandelbaum; Kane/Miller, 1990
Grandma's Baseball by Gavin Curtis; Crown Publishers, 1990
Shoes From Grandpa by Mem Fox; Orchard, 1989
Daddy, play with me! by Shigeo Watanabe; Philomel Books, 1984
Jamaica Tag-Along by Juanita Havill; Houghton Mifflin, 1989
Angel Child, Dragon Child by Michele Maria Surat; Scholastic Inc., 1983
Mei Li by Thomas Handford; Doubleday, 1939
Friday Night is Papa Night by Ruth A. Sonneborn; Puffin, 1970
What Mary Jo Shared by Janice Mary Uary; Scholastic Inc., 1983
A Chair for My Mother by Vera B. Williams; Greenwillow, 1982
More, More, More Said the Baby by Vera Williams; Greenwillow, 1990
Sachiko Means Happiness by Kimiko Sakai; Children's Press, 1991
On the Pampas by Maria Cristina Brusca; Holt, 1991
At the Crossroads by Rachel Isadora; Greenwillow, 1991
The Little Band by James Sage; Macmillan/Margaret K. McElderry, 1991
Con Mi Hermano With My Brother by Eileen Roe; Bradbury 1990
Peter's Pocket by Eve Rice; Greenwillow, 1989
How My Parents Learned to Eat by Ina Friedman; Houghton Mifflin, 1984

Nonfiction:

A Family in China by Nance Lui Fyson and Richard Greenhill; Lerner Publications, 1985
A Family in Nigeria by Carol Barker; Lerner Publications, 1985
(These are from a series of books on families from different lands.)
Hector Lives in the United States Now by Joan Hewett; Lippincott, 1990
The Sioux (A New True Book) by Childrens Press, 1984
Count Your Way Through India (part of a series) by Jim Hoskins; Carolrhoda, 1990
This is the way we go to school: A Book About Children Around the World by Edithe Baer; Scholastic Inc., 1990
An Aboriginal Family by Rolio Browne; Lerner Publications, 1985
Family in Australia by Emily Gimmer and Shirley McConkey; Bookwright, 1985
Loving by Ann Morris; Lothrop, 1990
All Kinds of Families by Norma Simon; Albert Whitman & Company, 1976
People and Homes by Carol Bowyer and Roma Trundle; Usborne, 1978

Center Activities

Families

Bulletin Board

Cover a bulletin board with blue butcher paper.

Use precut letters or write the heading using a wide felt marker.

Pin up pictures of children or families from various countries and cultural groups or you may put up one of the posters from this book.

Activities

Set a table in front of the bulletin board to hold activities and books.

1. Books
Put out a selection of fiction and nonfiction books for your students to enjoy. Change the books every week to keep interest high. (You will find many excellent selections listed in the bibliography on page 1.)

2. Puzzles
These may be puzzles of families or children which you have purchased or puzzles you have made yourself following these directions.

   a. Reproduce the puzzles on pages 45 through 48 on tag.
   b. Color the pictures.
   c. Laminate or cover them with clear Contact paper.
   d. Cut the puzzles apart and put them in large sturdy envelopes.

You can also make puzzles using pictures from magazines by gluing the picture to tag and following the same steps.

3. Paper Dolls

Make a set of paper dolls for the center by reproducing pages 41 through 44 on tag. Color the paper dolls and clothing, laminate or cover in clear Contact paper, and cut out all pieces. Store them in a sturdy box.

Children can use the paper dolls in pairs or small groups to encourage oral language and creative play.

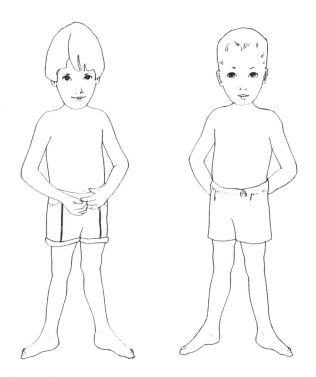

4. Sorting Circles

Help children explore differences of opinion about likes and dislikes by having them work in pairs to select and sort items.

Materials needed:
• magazine pictures (two of each item)
• two big overlapping circles of yarn
• box to hold the pictures

Directions for sorting:
a. Each child selects five items he/she likes from the set of pictures.

b. They then each place their pictures into the overlapping circles. Pictures of the same item go into the center, different items go into each child's own circle.

You may want to put out pictures of items in specific categories such as...

| colors | fruits and vegetables | types of toys |
| clothing | sports and games | animals |

Families

Family Names

Brainstorm with your students to name all of words we use for family members. If your students have begun to read put the words on a chart to keep up in class. List all the variations your children name. List non-English words if they are used by your students.

Mother	Mom	Mommy	Mama
Father	Dad	Daddy	Papa
Aunt	Uncle	Cousin	Niece
Nephew	Grandpa	Grandma	Tia

What is a family?

Help your students develop an understanding of what makes a family, both a birth family and the many variations on family that exist in our and other countries.

1. A family is a mother and father, brothers and sisters, and other relatives.

2. A family is made up of the people who love you and take care of you. (Depending on the age, maturity, and needs of your students, talk about adoptive families and families composed of different elements such as friends of one or both parents living in the household and helping care for the children.)

3. A family can be your all-the-time family or a for-a-while family. (Talk about foster families or families composed of relatives such as grandparents.)

Why do we need a family?

See how many ideas your children can come up with for why families are important. Explain to your students that these same reasons apply to families throughout the world. The age and maturity level of your students will determine the depth of the discussion. (Guide them to include elements such as love, care, safety, education, food, shelter, clothing, etc.)

Family Album

Buy or make a scrapbook to contain pictures about each of your students and his/her family. Allow a page for each child. Send a note home requesting one or more pictures of the family to go on the page. Return the pictures at the end of the school year.

Let's Learn About Families Around the World

Families Around the World - page 8

Give children an opportunity to tell what they think
families in other lands are like. Use the poster to show
pictures of families in other countries.

Family Homes - pages 9 and 10

Use the pictures on page 9 to help children understand that people
live in all kinds of different places and that these different habitats
determine the type of homes they need. Develop the vocabulary
needed to name the various types of homes (tent, house, apartment,
houseboat, trailer, condominium, hut, etc.) and building materials (brick,
stone, mud, wood, etc).

Add some fun to this discussion by reading your favorite version of *The Three Little
Pigs* to the class. Discuss the types of materials the pigs used to construct their homes.

Reproduce page 10 for children to draw their own home. Have them dictate or write to
complete these sentences.

> This is <u>Annie</u>'s home.
> It is a <u>house</u>.

> This is <u>Tay</u>'s home.
> It is a <u>trailer</u>.

> This is <u>Marco</u>'s home.
> It is an apartment.

> This is <u>Fawn</u>'s home.
> It is a <u>condominium</u>.

Clothing - pages 11 and 12

Use the pictures on page 11 to help children understand that clothing
in different parts of the world may be the same as they wear or may be
different because of weather or custom.

This is a good place to share a book such as *Hats, Hats, Hats* by Ann Morris which
shows hats around the world and their different functions or *Peter's Pocket* by Eve
Rice which tells of Peter's experiences wearing a pair of pants with no pockets.

Reproduce page 12 for children to match appropriate clothing to the weather or activity.

Food - pages 13 and 14

Use the pictures on page 13 to talk about the different types of food eaten around the world. Help children recognize similarities and differences with the foods their family eats. Talk about how we eat many foods here that are from other lands and cultures. Let children discuss what their families like to eat.

Have a "tasting picnic" to provide children with a chance to taste foods from a different country or culture.

Read books to students that show how a food can be used in different forms around the world.

> *Everybody Cooks Rice* by Norah Dooley; Carolrhoda Books, 1991
> *Bread, Bread, Bread* by Ann Morris; Lothrop, Lee & Shepard, 1989

Reproduce page 14 for children to mark the different types of food they have eaten.

School - page 15

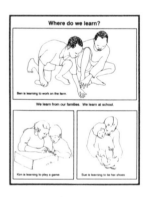

Talk about all of the ways children learn the things they need to know. See if they can tell you where they learn these things. Guide them to share what they learn from their families and what they learn when they go to school.

Give each child a large sheet of drawing paper. Have them fold the paper in half. On one half they are to draw something they have learned to do from their parents. On the other half they are to draw something they have learned to do at school. Have children dictate or write a sentence about each picture.

First graders will enjoy hearing you read *Crow Boy* (by Taro Yashima) and his school experiences.

Celebrations - pages 16 and 17

Use the symbols on page 16 to discuss the different occasions when families celebrate (birthdays, religious holidays, turning a certain age, promotions, Mother's Day, etc).

piñata - Posadas   evergreen tree - Christmas
menorah - Hanukkah   Maypole - May Day
pysanky egg - Easter
mkeka and kikombe cha umoja - Kwanzaa

Have children explain how their families celebrate special occasions.

Read books about different celebrations to your class. For example:

The Cobweb Christmas by Shirley Climo; Thomas Crowell, 1982
The Mother's Day Mice by Eve Bunting; Clarion, 1986
Latkes and Applesauce by Fran Manushkin; Scholastic Inc.,1990
Rosa by Leo Politi; Charles Scribner's Sons, 1963
Fourth of July by Barbara Joosse; Knopf, 1985
Fiesta by June Behrens; Children's Press, 1978
Mary McLean and the St. Patrick's Day Parade by Steven Kroll; Scholastic Inc.,1991

Reproduce page 17 for each child. Have them make a picture of their favorite celebration. Children who are writing may write a paragraph describing the event.

Families - page 18

Read *All Kinds of Families* by Norma Simon.

Discuss the different sizes and make-up of the families shown on page 18. You may also use the poster which shows different family groupings.

Use the story and page to help children understand that no matter how different another family may seem from their own, they all have the same basic function: to love, respect, and care for one another.

Pages 19 through 23 contain pictures of children from different countries. Use this for further discussion of likenesses and differences among families. Help children locate the countries on a world map.

Families Around the World

Families live in all the countries of the world.
These families are like my family in some ways.
These families are different than my family in some ways.

Family Homes

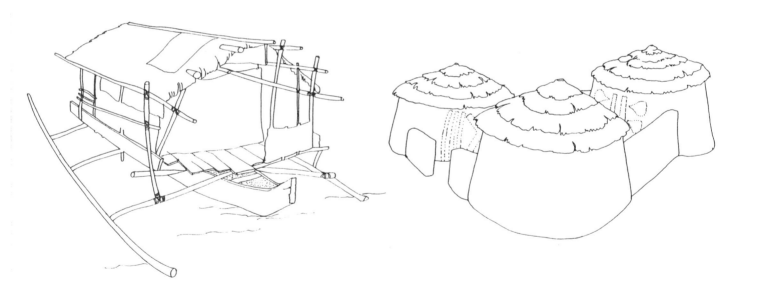

Families live in homes.
There are many kinds of homes.
These homes have different names.

Do you live in a home like any of these?

This is _____'s home.

It is a _____.

Clothing

Families have clothes for work.
Families have clothes for play.
Families have clothes for different weather.
Families have clothes for special days.

 Families Around the World

Note: Have children cut out the correct clothing for the weather shown.

What do you wear on a _____ day?

Family Meals

All families must eat to be strong and healthy.
They eat bread and meat.
They eat fruits and vegetables.
Some of these are the same foods we eat.
Some of these are different than what we eat.

Have you ever eaten the foods on this page?

Families Around the World

Note: Have children color the foods they have tasted. Have them circle the ones they like and underline the ones they dislike.

What foods do you eat?

Where do we learn?

Ben is learning to work on the farm.

We learn from our families. We learn at school.

Kim is learning to play a game.

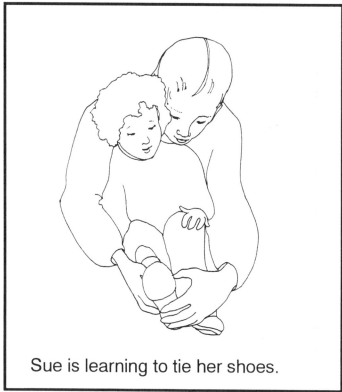

Sue is learning to tie her shoes.

Families Around the World

Family Celebrations

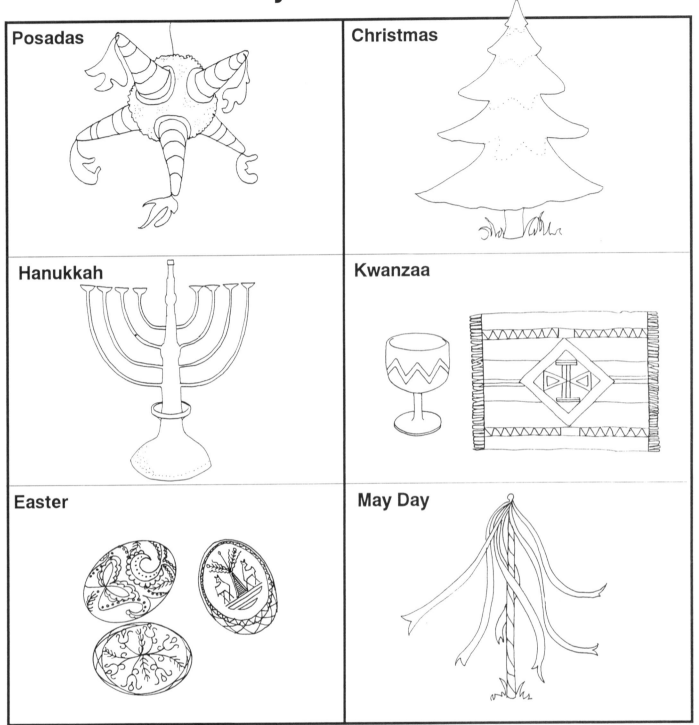

Posadas

Christmas

Hanukkah

Kwanzaa

Easter

May Day

Families celebrate special days.
They may celebrate at home.
They may celebrate at church.
They may celebrate with the whole town.

Note: Have children draw a picture of an event celebrated in their home.

My Family Celebrates

17

Families

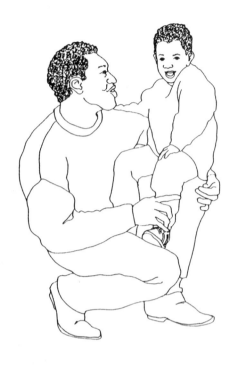 

Families come in different sizes.
Some are big and some are small.
Families don't all have the same people in them.

A family is those people who love you.
They take the best care of you they can.
They keep you safe from harm.

 Families Around the World

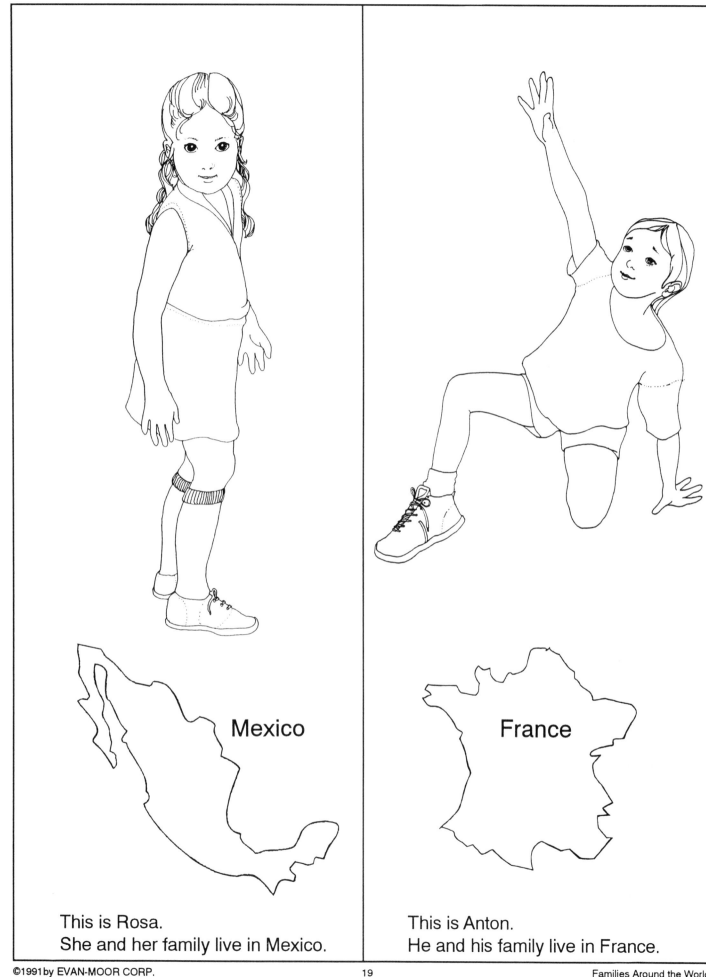

Mexico

France

This is Rosa.
She and her family live in Mexico.

This is Anton.
He and his family live in France.

China

This is Chun Ling.
She and her family live in China.

Italy

This is Anna.
She and her family live in Italy.

Note: Reproduce a copy for each child in your class to color.

Nigeria

This is John.
He and his family live in Nigeria.

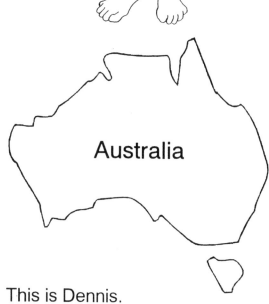

Australia

This is Dennis.
He and his family live in Australia.

Families Around the World

_____'s Family

This is my family.
We live in _____.

Most countries have families of all kinds.
They are alike in some ways.
They are different in some ways.

These families look different from each other.
But they are all Americans.

What country is your family from?

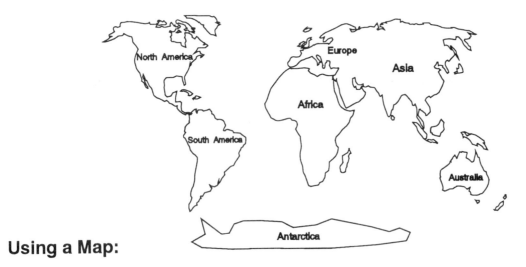

Using a Map:

Introduce your students to maps and globes as you study families around the world. Have a globe and a large, simple world map available.

When you read a story about a child or family from another country show children where that country is located on the globe and/or map.

Send home the letter and form on page 25 to be filled out by the child and his/her parents. Use this information to mark birthplaces on the world map.

Invite Speakers:

One way to expose your students to the vast cultural diversity in our country is to have speakers come to share with the class. The speakers may be parents or grandparent of your students or they may be speakers from the community.

Be sure the speaker understands the age and maturation level of your students so she/ he can speak appropriately.

Encourage the speaker to talk about everyday life.

> What does the country look like?
> What is family life like?
> What games do you play?
> What do you eat?
> Is your clothing different than in our country?
> What kinds of pets do you have?

Encourage the speaker to bring in pictures and artifacts from the country or culture.

Remind the speaker of the short attention span of young children. Keep it interesting and keep it short!
Reproduce the form on page 25 to send home to parents.

Dear Parents,

We are learning about families all over the world. We want to know more about our own families and where they came from. We are going to find these places on a world map. Please help by filling in the form below. Return it to school by _____.

Thank you for your help.

Sincerely,

_____ was born in _____
(Child's name)   (Country)

His/Her mother was born in _____.
(Country)

His/Her father was born in _____.
(Country)

- -

Dear Parents,

We are learning about families all over the world. We want to know more about our own families and where they came from. If you or someone in your family would be willing to speak to our class about family life in an-other country please indicate below. I will be in contact with you about a day and time. Return the form to school by _____.

Thank you for your help.

Sincerely,

___ Yes, I would like to speak to the class about family life in _____.
___ I am unable to speak to the class, but I know someone who would
    be able come.
___ I am unable to speak to the class at this time.

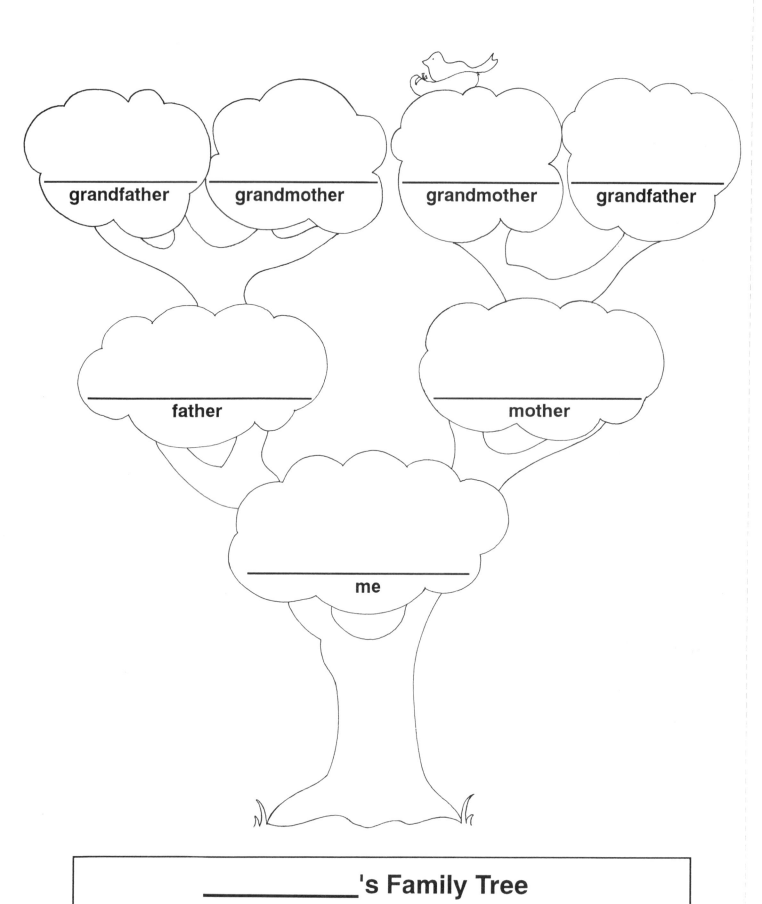

_____ grandfather _____ grandmother _____ grandmother _____ grandfather

_____ father _____ mother

_____ me

_____'s Family Tree

Paint a Big Book

This is an ongoing project since each child will be making several paintings. You will need to consider where pictures will be placed to dry and where they will be stored until they are put into a book.

Getting Ready:

Set up the easels for painting. If your classroom has carpeted floors be sure to place a sheet of plastic or oilcloth under the easels.

Prepare the paint, brushes, and paper (large sheets of painting or butcher paper). Place these items in an easily accessible place if children are to be responsible for collecting their own materials.

Discuss the topics children will be painting. You may want to assign one painting assignment per day or week (depending on the number of students in your class).

  a. house
  b. family
  c. pets
  d. working together
  e. playing together
  f. own choice (food, game, vacation, etc.)

Big Book Pages:

Children paint their pictures. After the pictures dry, they write (or dictate) a sentence either on the painting itself or on a sheet of lined paper which is then attached to the painting.

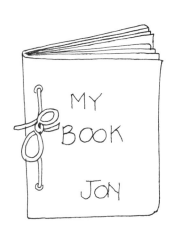

When all of a child's paintings are completed and dry and the writing is completed, put them together with a butcher paper cover to create the child's own "big book."

Putting the Book Together:

Have the child put his/her pages together in the order he/she wishes. Put the pages between the cover sheets and staple them together on the left side. Cover the staples with cloth tape to protect little fingers from staple cuts. Or punch holes through the pages and lace the book together with yarn.

Provide time for each child to share his/her book with the class, then place them in a display area so others can read them.

Family Finger Plays and Clapping Rhymes

Fingerplays:

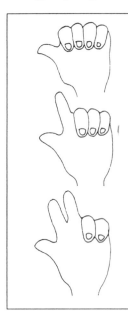

This is my mother

This is my father

This is my brother tall

This is my sister

This is our baby

Oh how I love them all

Curl fingers in as you say this line

Clapping Rhymes:

A Big Family

Fa - ther and Mo - ther

Sis - ters and bro - ther

Two grand - fa - thers

And one grand - mo - ther

Wait!
There's more!

Lots of Aunt - ies

Lots of Un - cles

Cou - sins, cou - sins

By the do - zens

A Little Family

My mom and me

Just two to see

Hap - py as can be

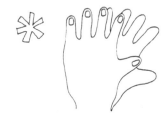

Songs and Games

Places Families Live

Sing and play that old game 'Round the Village. Sing the verse to the tune of *Go In and Out the Window*. Change the place to city, country, barnyard, forest, etc.

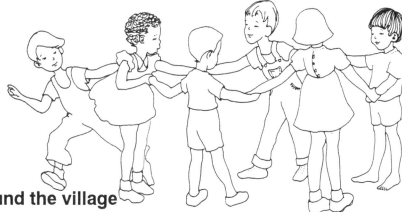

Verse 1

> **Go 'round and 'round the village**
> **Go 'round and 'round the village**
> **Go 'round and 'round the village**
> **As we have done before.**

Verse 2 - Go in and out the window...
Verse 3 - Now come and face your partner...
Verse 4 - Now follow me to London (change city name to fit country)...

Directions for game:

Children stand in a circle holding hands. "It" stands outside the circle.
As children sing the verse "It" follows the directions below.

Verse 1 - "It" skips or runs around circle.
Verse 2 - Children in circle raise arms to form arches while "It" weaves in and out.
Verse 3 - "It" chooses a partner and stands facing him.
Verse 4 - "It" leads partner in and out of circle.
Verse 5 - "It" returns to circle and partner becomes "It."

Clothing People Wear

Sing this old folk song.

> **Mary wore her red dress, red dress, red dress**
> **Mary wore her red dress all day long.**

Change the child's name, the color, and the piece of wearing apparel with each verse.

Using pictures from story books and magazines, sing the song again adding clothing from other cultures.

> Reiko wore a kimono...
> Toby wore a plaid kilt...

 Families Around the World

Language

Family Circle

Have children sit in a circle. Assign a topic and have each child in the circle share an answer about his/her family. Allow children the option of saying "pass."

- number of family members
- who does what work at home
- favorite TV show to watch together
- favorite food of family
- family pets
- favorite thing to do together
- languages spoken at home
- type of home family lives in

My Favorite Relative

Have each child draw a picture of a favorite family member. They then show the picture to the class and explain why they like this person so much.

A Little Book about My Family

Staple together ten small sheets of drawing paper inside a cover of construction paper. Each child can select what they wish to include in the book, but it must have something to do with their family. Have suggestions ready for your slow starters.

family members	house	car
pets	favorite food	celebrations
vacations	games play together	TV shows

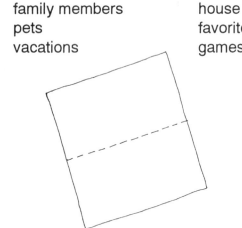

Note: Reproduce the "cookie cutter people" patterns on page 34 to use with these activities. Cut them out of felt or Pellon if you wish to use them on a flannel board.

Math

Counting

1. Place a pile of cookie cutter people where your students can reach them. Have each child pick out shapes to represent everyone in their family, paste the shapes to a sheet of construction paper, and write the number of people they have shown in the corner of the paper.

2. Place a row of cookie cutter people where the children can see them. Have them count the shapes in a variety of ways.

   How many people do you see standing in this row?
   How many boys/girls do you see?
   Are there any babies in this row?

Repeat the activity using different numbers and configurations of people.

Graphing

1. Graph the number of boys and girls in the classroom.

   Make a simple graph form on a large sheet of butcher paper.
   Put out a pile of cookie cutter people shapes.
   Have each child select the shape that represents him/herself and place it on the graph.

   Ask questions about the finished graph.

   How many boys are in our room?
   How many girls are in our room?
   Are there more boys or more girls?

BOYS   GIRLS

Patterning

Reproduce the cookie cutter people in different colors.
Use the different sizes and colors to practice patterning.

1. Lay out a pattern. Have children copy the pattern exactly. Begin with simple patterns. Create more complicated ones as they are able to succeed with the simple ones.

2. Lay out a pattern. Have children continue the pattern.

3. Have children create a pattern for their classmates to copy.

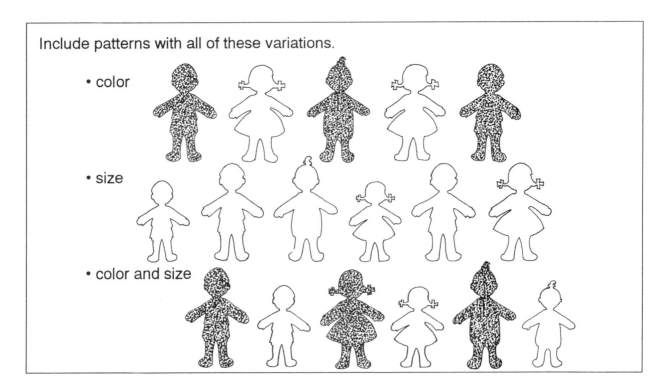

Counting in Other Languages

Invite children who speak another language to teach the class how to count to ten (or higher) in that language.

Share counting books from the series *Count Your Way Through* (country's name) published by Carolrhoda.

Math with My Family

Dear Parents,

We are learning many math skills at school. You can help your child practice these skills at home. Here are some ideas you might try.

1. Counting

Have your child count to find out how many _____ you have in your home.

rooms	windows	doors	chairs
light switches	clocks	people	pets

Have your child count out loud as high as he/she can go.

2. Geometric Shapes

Have your child find objects around the house that have these shapes:

square   rectangle   circle   triangle

Ask your child to tell how many sides and how many corners each shape has.

3. Measurement

Give your child a ruler. Have him/her measure common items around the house (pencil, knife, hairbrush, etc). Give help when it is needed.

Use a measuring tape to help your child measure family members.

height	waist	length of feet
wrist	ankle	etc.

Thank you for your support.

Sincerely,

Cookie Cutter People Patterns

Note: Stories can be a valuable tool for teaching many skills. Favorite books can be read many times. Here are three activities to do on different days with this story.

Shoes From Grandpa
by Mem Fox

Day 1

Read Shoes From Grandpa.

This story takes place in Australia. You may want to show your children where Australia is located on a map or globe.

Develop Vocabulary - Using the illustrations on each page help children learn the names of all the different types of wearing apparel. Practice descriptive words at the same time.

Play "I'm Wearing" - Children all sit in a circle. Teacher names a piece of clothing. Everyone who is wearing that item stands up. Have each child standing say something to describe the item.

"I am wearing a red blouse."
"My blouse has ruffles on the sleeves."
"I have a green blouse with long sleeves."

Day 2

Read Shoes From Grandpa.

Have children recall what each relative gave Jessie.

Grandpa (shoes)	Dad (socks)
Mom (skirt)	Cousin (blouse)
Sister (sweater)	Grandma (coat)
Aunt (scarf)	Brother (hat)
Uncle (mittens)	

Ask "What did Jessie want that she didn't get from her relatives?" (blue jeans)

Day 3

Read Shoes From Grandpa.

Jessie got funny bunny mittens and a silly crocodile hat that made her laugh. Reproduce the form on page 36 for each child. Have them create a silly hat and funny mittens on the blank shapes.

Funny Mittens and a Hat to Make You Laugh!

Note: Stories can be a valuable tool for teaching many skills. Favorite books can be read many times. Here are three activities to do on different days with this story.

At the Crossroads
by Rachel Isadora

Day 1

Read *At the Crossroads*.

This story takes place in South Africa. You may want to show your students where this is located on a large map or globe.

Help children recall information by asking questions such as these.

> Who are the children waiting for?
> Where have their fathers been?
> What do the children sing?
> How long do the children have to wait?
> How do the fathers get home from the mines?

Day 2

Read *At the Crossroads*.

Use the illustrations to see what life is like in this village. Help your children compare and contrast this way of life with their own.

buildings	water source	school
transportation	musical instruments	clothing
parent's jobs	taking a bath	

Day 3

Read *At the Crossroads*.

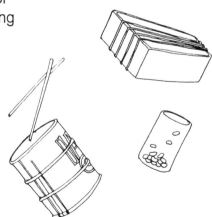

Make instruments out of boxes and cans. (See page 38.)

March around the classroom singing.

A "Homemade" Band

You will need:

- shoe boxes
- large rubber bands
- large cans with lids
- small cans with lids
- sticks (for drumsticks)
- pebbles

Shoe Box Guitars

Wrap one or more rubber bands around a shoe box. You will get a different sound from rubber bands of different lengths and thicknesses. Pluck the rubber bands to create music.

Can Drums

Place the plastic lid on the can. Hit the lid with a sturdy stick. Sounds will vary depending on the size of the can and the stick used as a drumstick.

Shakers

Put some pebbles (or rice, beans, etc.) into a small can. Place the lid securely on the can. Shake the can to create a musical sound. The sound will vary depending on the size of the can, the size of the pebbles, and the fullness of the can.

Note: Stories can be a valuable tool for teaching many skills. Favorite books can be read many times. Here are three activities to do on different days with this story.

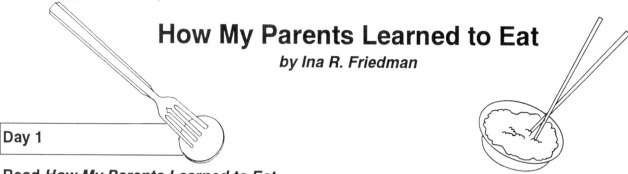

How My Parents Learned to Eat
by Ina R. Friedman

Day 1

Read *How My Parents Learned to Eat*.

This story takes place in Japan. You may want to show your students where this is located on a large map or globe.

Help children recall information by asking questions such as these.

> Where did Aiko live?
> Where did she meet the sailor John?
> Why didn't John invite Aiko to dinner?
> Who helped John learn how to use chopsticks?
> Who helped Aiko learn to use a knife and fork?
> What is different between the way Americans use a knife and fork
> and the way English people use a knife and fork?

Day 2

Read *How My Parents Learned to Eat*.

Use the illustrations to see what life is like in Japan. Help your children compare and contrast this way of life with their own.

clothing	buildings	restaurants
eating utensils	signs	beds

Reproduce the cut and paste activity on page 40 for each child. Explain to children that they are to paste the pictures by the child in whose country you would <u>usually</u> find the item.

Day 3

Read *How My Parents Learned to Eat*.

Learn to use chopsticks. You can often buy inexpensive wooden chopsticks in the foreign food section of your supermarket. Invite several parents (who can use chopsticks) to come in and help on the day of the lesson. Give each child a small dish of sticky rice with which to practice. Remind them that it isn't easy to learn to use chopsticks. This is just a chance to try different eating utensils. Make it a fun experience, not a chore.

Japan and the USA

40

いろは

a b c

Note: Reproduce these paper dolls on construction paper or tag. Also reproduce the clothing on pages 43 and 44 for your students to use to dress the paper doll children on pages 41 and 42.

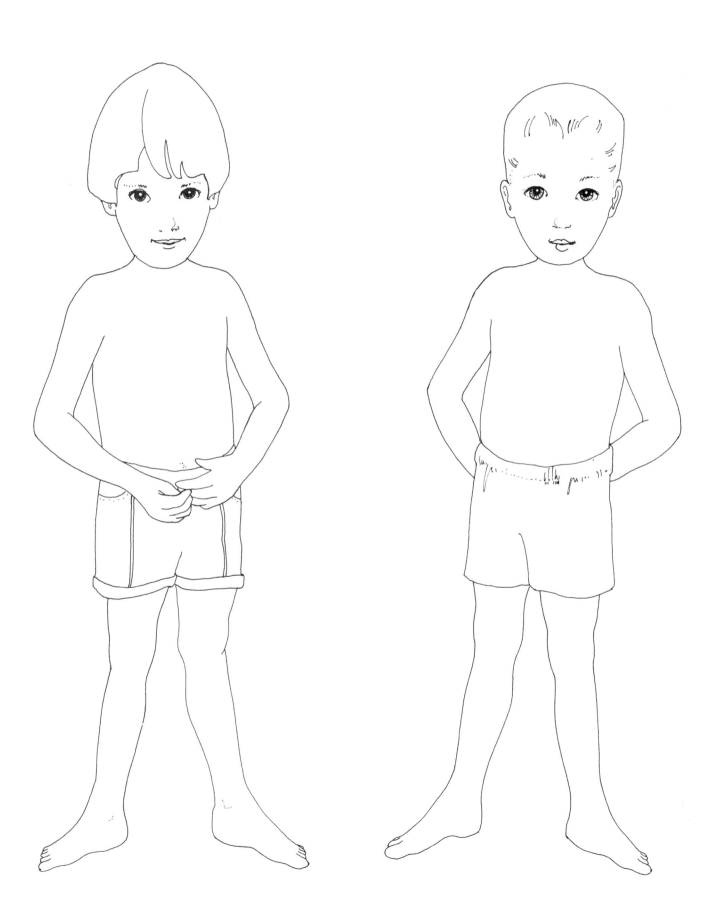

Families Around the World

Note: Reproduce these paper dolls on construction paper or tag. Also reproduce the clothing on pages 43 and 44 for your students to use to dress the paper doll children on pages 41 and 42.

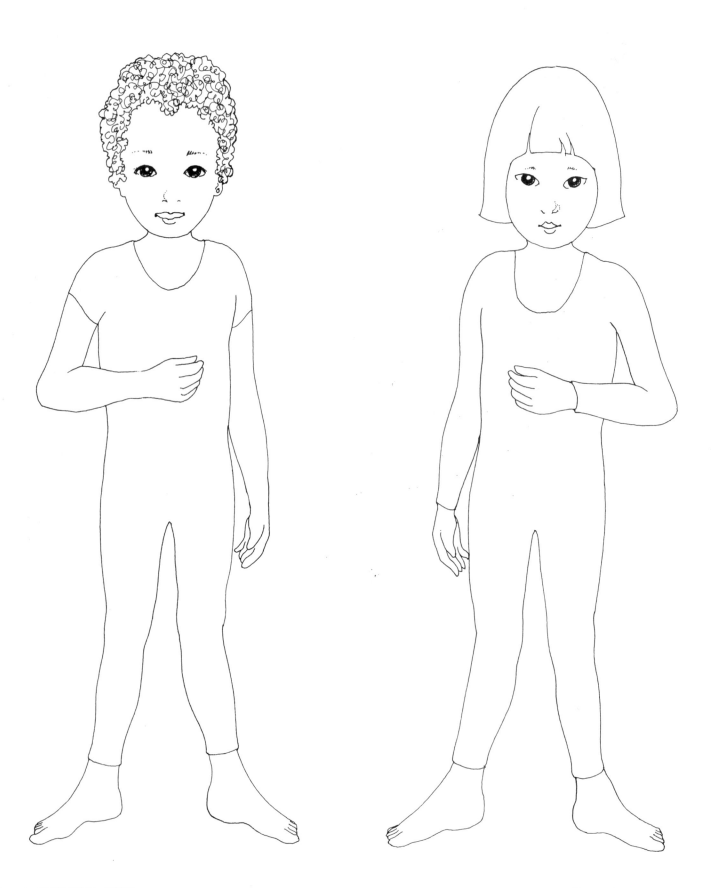

Families Around the World

Note: Reproduce this clothing on construction paper.

Families Around the World

Note: Reproduce this clothing on construction paper.

44

Note: Each child will need this puzzle and a blank sheet of paper on which to paste it.

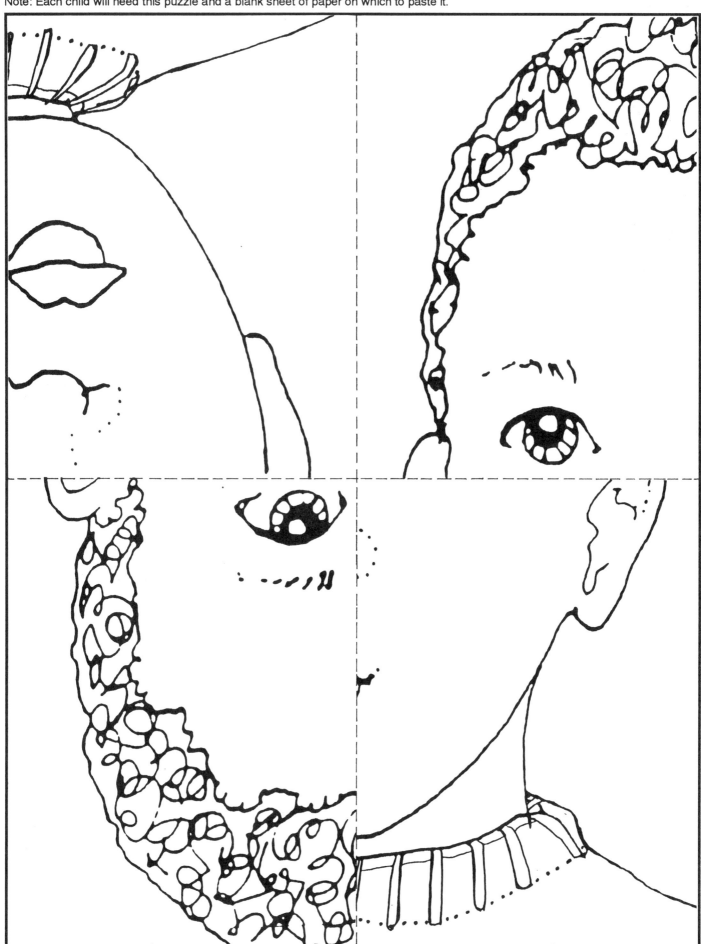

45

Families Around the World

Note: Each child will need this puzzle and a blank sheet of paper on which to paste it.

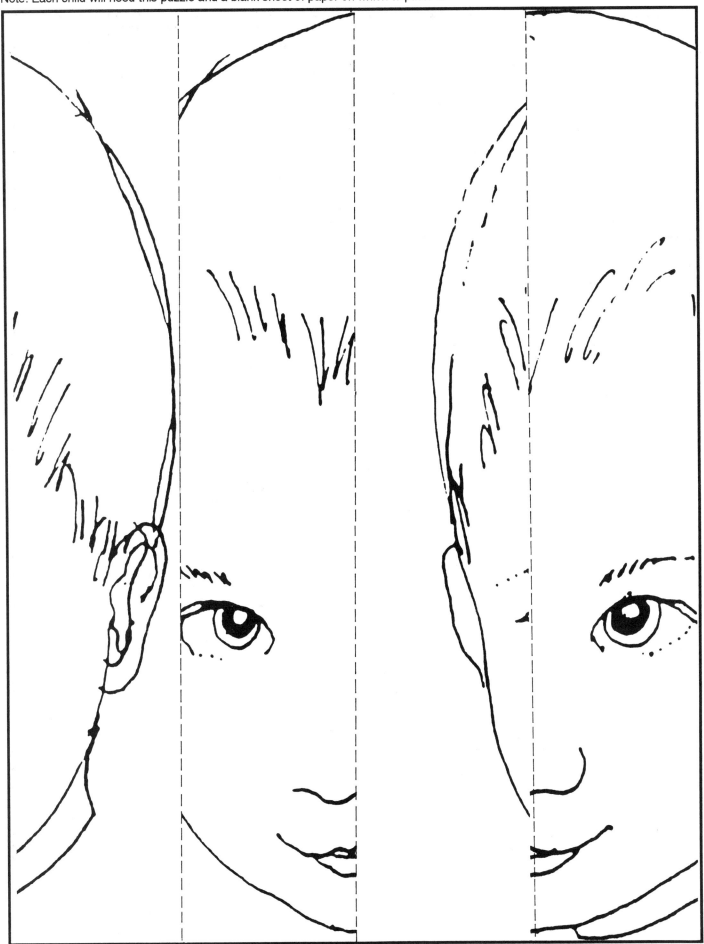

Families Around the World

48